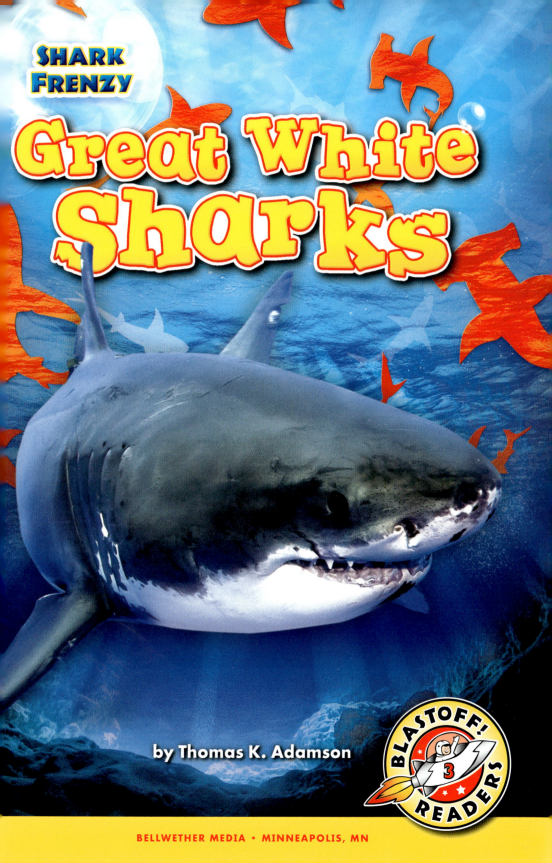

Great White Sharks

SHARK FRENZY

by Thomas K. Adamson

BELLWETHER MEDIA • MINNEAPOLIS, MN

Blastoff! Readers are carefully developed by literacy experts to build reading stamina and move students toward fluency by combining standards-based content with developmentally appropriate text.

LEVELS

Level 1 provides the most support through repetition of high-frequency words, light text, predictable sentence patterns, and strong visual support.

Level 2 offers early readers a bit more challenge through varied sentences, increased text load, and text-supportive special features.

Level 3 advances early-fluent readers toward fluency through increased text load, less reliance on photos, advancing concepts, longer sentences, and more complex special features.

★ **Blastoff! Universe**

Reading Level

Grade K

Grades 1–3

Grade 4

This edition first published in 2021 by Bellwether Media, Inc.

No part of this publication may be reproduced in whole or in part without written permission of the publisher. For information regarding permission, write to Bellwether Media, Inc., Attention: Permissions Department, 6012 Blue Circle Drive, Minnetonka, MN 55343.

Library of Congress Cataloging-in-Publication Data

Names: Adamson, Thomas K., 1970- author.
Title: Great white sharks / by Thomas K. Adamson.
Description: Minneapolis, MN : Bellwether Media, Inc., [2021] | Series: Blastoff! Readers: Shark frenzy | Includes bibliographical references and index. | Audience: Ages 5-8 | Audience: Grades 2-3 | Summary: "Simple text and full-color photography introduce beginning readers to great white sharks. Developed by literacy experts for students in kindergarten through third grade"- Provided by publisher.
Identifiers: LCCN 2020001626 (print) | LCCN 2020001627 (ebook) | ISBN 9781644872451 (library binding) | ISBN 9781681037080 (ebook)
Subjects: LCSH: White shark-Juvenile literature.
Classification: LCC QL638.95.L3 A333 2021 (print) | LCC QL638.95.L3 (ebook) | DDC 597.3/3-dc23
LC record available at https://lccn.loc.gov/2020001626
LC ebook record available at https://lccn.loc.gov/2020001627

Text copyright © 2021 by Bellwether Media, Inc. BLASTOFF! READERS and associated logos are trademarks and/or registered trademarks of Bellwether Media, Inc.

Editor: Rebecca Sabelko   Designer: Kathleen Petelinsek

Printed in the United States of America, North Mankato, MN.

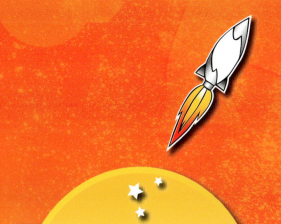

Table of Contents

What Are Great White Sharks?	4
Scary Smiles	8
Sneak Attack!	14
Deep Dive on the Great White Shark	20
Glossary	22
To Learn More	23
Index	24

What Are Great White Sharks?

Great white sharks are named for their white bellies.

These feared hunters swim all over the world. They spend time in coastal waters and deep **currents**.

Great White Shark Range

range =

Great whites are **vulnerable**. Many people catch these sharks for their fins and teeth. Great whites also get caught in nets that keep beaches safe.

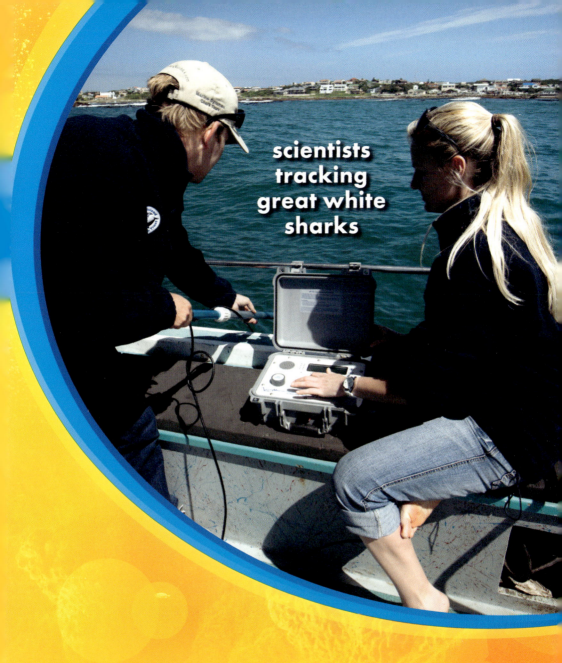

scientists tracking great white sharks

Scientists track the sharks to learn more about how they live. They make plans to help keep the sharks safe.

Scary Smiles

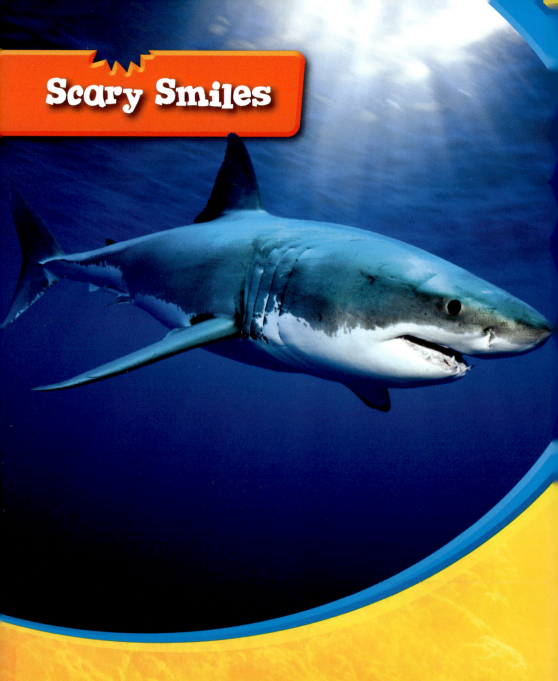

Great white sharks are built to be **fearsome** ocean hunters.

Their **torpedo-shaped** bodies can grow up to 20 feet (6 meters) long. Their strong tails help them make quick attacks.

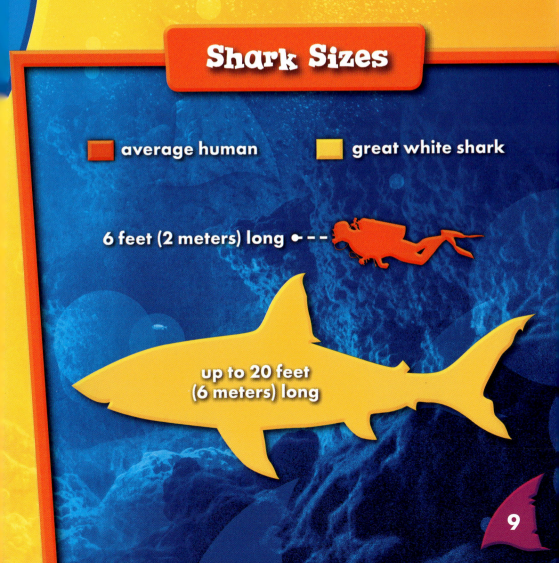

Shark Sizes

- average human: 6 feet (2 meters) long
- great white shark: up to 20 feet (6 meters) long

Great whites have over 300 triangle-shaped teeth. Each **serrated** tooth is like the edge of a saw.

Great whites' teeth tear **prey** apart. Their jaws and teeth are strong enough to bite through bone!

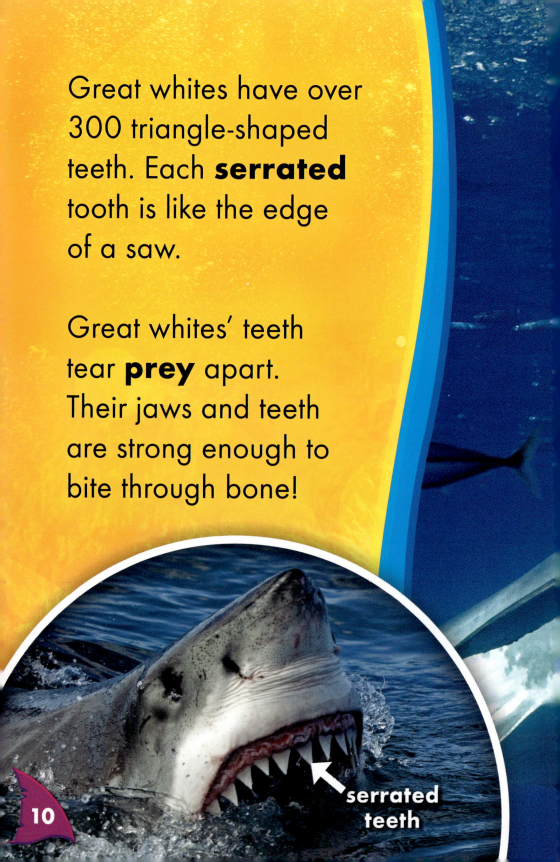

serrated teeth

The coloring on great white sharks acts as **camouflage**. They are hard to see from above and below.

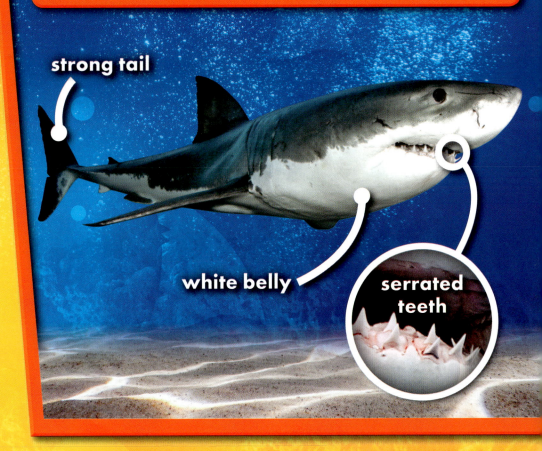

Identify a Great White Shark
- strong tail
- white belly
- serrated teeth

Their gray backs are hard to spot against the seafloor. Their light bellies are hard to see against the bright surface water.

Sneak Attack!

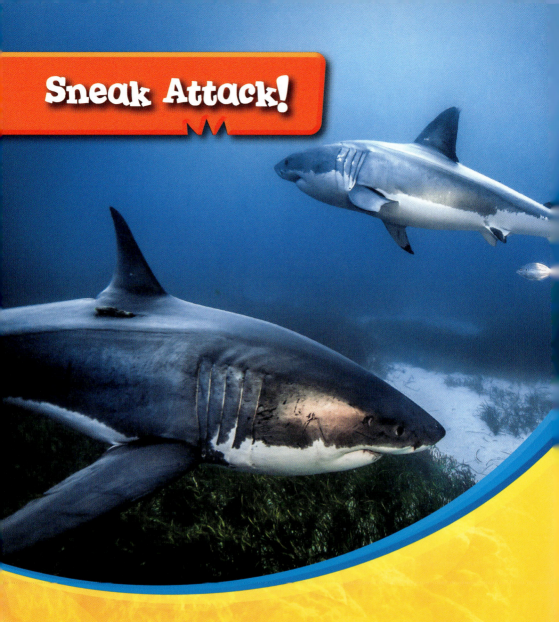

Great whites are active during the day and at night. They usually live alone. But they will hunt in small groups.

Great white sharks eat seals, sea lions, dolphins, and dead whales. They also hunt smaller sharks and sea turtles.

Great White Shark Diet

sea lions

seals

dolphins

Great white sharks **ambush** their prey from below. They race toward their meal. Then they ram into the animal. Sometimes the sharks jump out of the water!

These **predators** eat their meals with quick, large bites.

Great white sharks have few enemies. **Orcas** are the only animals known to attack great whites. No other ocean creatures dare to try.

Great whites are mighty **apex predators** of the sea!

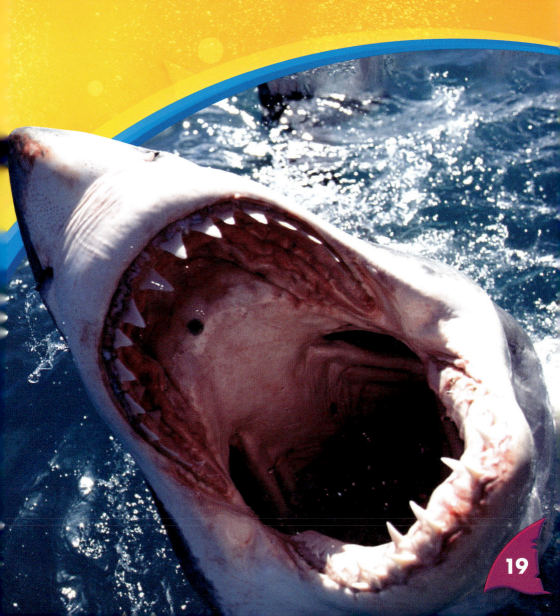

Deep Dive on the Great White Shark

strong tail

LIFE SPAN:
up to **30 years**

LENGTH:
up to **20 feet (6 meters) long**

WEIGHT:
up to **4,000 pounds (1,800 kilograms)**

TOP SPEED:
up to **35 miles (56 kilometers) per hour**

DEPTH RANGE:
up to **3,900 feet (1,200 meters)**

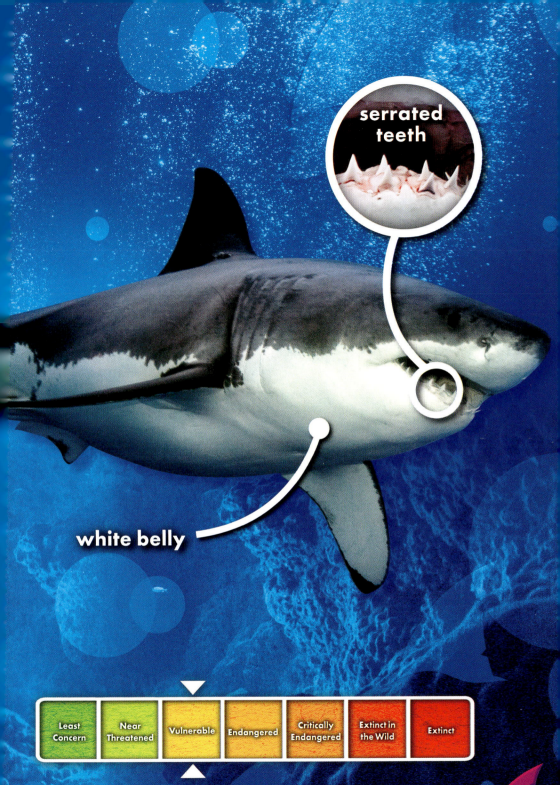

Glossary

ambush—to attack from a hiding place

apex predators—animals at the top of the food chain that are not preyed upon by other animals

camouflage—a way of using color to blend in with surroundings

currents—patterns of water movement in a body of water

fearsome—very frightening or scary

orcas—killer whales

predators—animals that hunt other animals for food

prey—animals that are hunted by other animals for food

serrated—having a sawlike edge

torpedo-shaped—having a tube shape like a torpedo; torpedoes are weapons fired underwater.

vulnerable—likely to become endangered; endangered animals are in danger of dying out.

To Learn More

AT THE LIBRARY

Adamson, Thomas K. *Great White Shark vs. Killer Whale*. Minneapolis, Minn.: Bellwether Media, 2020.

Donohue, Moira Rose. *Great White Sharks*. New York, N.Y.: Children's Press, 2018.

Skerry, Brian. *The Ultimate Book of Sharks: Your Guide to These Fierce and Fantastic Fish*. Washington, D.C.: National Geographic, 2018.

ON THE WEB

FACTSURFER

Factsurfer.com gives you a safe, fun way to find more information.

1. Go to www.factsurfer.com.
2. Enter "great white sharks" into the search box and click 🔍.
3. Select your book cover to see a list of related content.

Index

ambush, 16
apex predators, 19
backs, 13
bellies, 4, 13
bite, 10, 17
bodies, 9
camouflage, 12
color, 4, 12, 13
currents, 5
deep dive, 20-21
fins, 6
hunters, 5, 8, 14, 15
jaws, 10
name, 4
nets, 6
ocean, 8, 18
orcas, 18
predators, 17
prey, 10, 15, 16, 17

range, 5
scientists, 7
size, 9
status, 6
swim, 5
tails, 9, 13
teeth, 6, 10, 13
track, 7
waters, 5, 13, 16

The images in this book are reproduced through the courtesy of: VisionDive, front cover; Andrea Izzotti, pp. 3, 20-21; wildestanimal, pp. 4-5, 18; atese, p. 6; robertharding/ Alamy, p. 7; Reinhard Dirscherl/ Alamy, pp. 8-9; Martin Prochazkacz, p. 10 (inset); ShaneMyersPhoto, pp. 10-11; Willyam Bradberry, p. 12; Tomas Kotouc, p. 13 (great white shark); WaterFrame/ Alamy, pp. 13 (serrated teeth), 21 (serrated teeth); Brad Leue/ Alamy, pp. 14-15; chbaum, p. 15 (sea lions); wim claes, p. 15 (seals); Zorro Stock Images, p. 15 (dolphins); Sergey Uryadnikov, pp. 16-17, 17; Brandon Cole Marine Photography/ Alamy, pp. 18-19; Marc Henauer, p. 22.